Marlene Dietrich

Designed by Gillian Greenwood

Dietrich by Alexandra de Lazareff

John Kobal

Marlene Dietrich

studio vista|dutton pictureback
general editor David Herbert

Acknowledgements

Most of the stills used are from the author's private collection, but thanks for the others are due to Miss Betty Leese of the National Film Archive, to Janus Barfoed of the Danish Film Archive, to Dr F. Güttinger, who also helped in the compilation of the early part of the filmography, and to Marc Ricci's Memory Shop. The author also wishes to thank Ray Durgnat, Kevin Brownlow, Mark Shivas, and Ian Wright for their help and advice in preparation of the manuscript and Anne Kilborn for her patience.

The extracts from *Fun in a Chinese Laundry* by Josef von Sternberg are reprinted by permission of Secker & Warburg, London, and the Macmillan Publishing Co., New York.

Stills are reproduced by courtesy of the following: Universal, 20th Century-Fox, Warner Bros., Paramount, United Artists, London Films, Columbia.

© John Kobal 1968
Published in London by Studio Vista Limited
Blue Star House, Highgate Hill, N 19
and in New York by E. P. Dutton and Co Inc
201 Park Avenue South, New York 3, NY
Distributed in Canada by General Publishing Co Ltd
30 Lesmill Road, Don Mills, Ontario
Set in 8D on 9 pt Univers, 2 pts leaded
Made and printed in Great Britain by
Richard Clay (The Chaucer Press), Ltd,
Bungay, Suffolk

SBN 289 37022 1 (paperback)
SBN 289 37024 8 (hardback)

Contents

Photographed by the Imperial Court Photographer 1904–5

Marlene Dietrich belongs to a generation that never cared to reveal its age.

Legend says she was born in Imperial Berlin sometime between 1901 and 1908; Marlene herself, with a touch of the 'gallows humour' ascribed to her by Hemingway, simply answers: 'Just say I'm 75 and let it go at that.'

But few people have. Arthur Knight made a brave attempt at establishing a date in 'Notes on a living legend' (*Films in Review*, December 1954): 'According to some accounts, she was born Maria Magdalene Dietrich, daughter of Louis Dietrich, a lieutenant, later major, in the Uhlan Cavalry. When he died, the story continues, her mother married Col. Edward von Losch of the famous Hussars. Another version eliminates Major Dietrich and reduces von Losch to lieutenant. In one biography Dietrich *père* retires after World War I, in another he dies on the Russian Front; von Losch dies variously on the Russian Front in 1915, or in Germany shortly before the end of World War I. Dietrich's mother is either of French descent, or "daughter of the head of the great Conrad Felsing jewelry firm", a concern founded by Marlene's great-grandfather which carried in its window the legend: "Purveyor to His Majesty the Kaiser".'

A birth certificate produced in Berlin, and quoted in the *New York Herald Tribune*, unflinchingly states that she was born on 27 December 1901 and that her father was Erich Otto Dietrich, a lieutenant, not in the cavalry but in the less romantic Royal Prussian Police.

Dietrich herself seems to have been silent about her parents and sister, although in one of her rare interviews (given to *Pour Nous* and printed in February 1931) she did talk about her ambition to play the violin: 'Actually I wanted to be a concert violinist. I spent my whole youth working with that goal in mind. My father was an officer, and we moved a great deal as a result. But I was always very persistent when I wanted to achieve a thing. At sixteen years of age, I used to practise six hours a day and was about to make my first public appearance in concert. And it would happen that at just that time I suffered a muscle damage, so that my arm couldn't be moved for a time. When I was finally well again, the Doctor forbade me to play any difficult pieces. This made a career as a concert violinist unthinkable and unbearable

7

for me. I gave up completely. . . . I read and read, and there was no end to the books I wanted to read. One day I came upon a section in a book by a German poet, which I found unspeakably beautiful. I read it out loud, and the music of the words made the text even more fascinating. Around that time I began to think seriously about a theatrical career, and as soon as I returned to Berlin, I tried for an audition with Reinhardt. I succeeded, and read him that section which had so enraptured me in Weimar. He gave me a chance, and after I overcame some difficulties from my parents' side, I was allowed to appear in a small scene on stage.

'In the following two years nothing much happened. At last, I got a part in *Broadway* (a musical in which she sang two songs). Through it I was discovered for operetta. Then I began to play in small films, to sing and to dance. Then came the film *Ich Küsse*

Broadway Guyl, Lennartz, Dietrich, Ander, Albu, Kupfer 1926

Ihre Hand, Madame (*I Kiss your Hand, Madam*) ; then *Die Frau nach der man sich sehnt*, or *Drei Lieben* (*Three Loves*) . . . the critics accused me of not opening my eyes enough, but I was supposed to be photogenic. . . . In between films I returned to the stage. That is where von Sternberg discovered me, when he came to Berlin, to search for a Lola for the film *The Blue Angel*.'

Dietrich began her acting career in Max Reinhardt's drama school in 1921. During her time there she met Rudolf Sieber, then a young assistant director, who was at the school looking for girls to appear as cocottes in a film party scene. Marlene was hired. According to August Scherl, 'That evening she sat down to sew herself an outlandish cocotte's dress from green brocade, and arrived the following morning, her hair styled with bacchanalian looseness and a monocle clenched in her eye.'

Die Frau nach der man sich sehnt, with Fritz Kortner

Small film and stage parts followed. One was a brief appearance in *Die Freudlose Gasse*, which included among its stars the actress she was later to be compared with : Greta Garbo. In 1925 she married Sieber and had a daughter, Maria, later that year. After her marriage, her life became more public and the facts become clearer. Yet opinions as to what happened, and when, still diverge. Dietrich has stated, for instance, that she was 'nothing in films until handled by von Sternberg'. She thus dismissed roughly seventeen films, although she had starred in several of them. Her attitude to her early work is reflected in von Sternberg's auto-biography *Fun in a Chinese Laundry* : 'She attached no value to it when I met her nor did she attach any value to anthying else as far as I could ascertain, with the exception of her baby daughter, musical saw, and some recordings by a singer called Whispering Jack Smith. She was inclined to jeer at herself and at others, though she was extremely loyal to her friends (many of whom were not always loyal to her), and quick to feel pity and to help those who flattered her for qualities that were not always flattering. She was frank and outspoken to a degree which might be termed tactless. Her personality was one of extreme sophistication and of an almost childish simplicity. . . . She was subject to severe depressions, these were balanced by periods of unbelievable vigour. To exhaust her was not possible; it was she who ex-hausted others and with enthusiasms few were able to share.'

Von Sternberg writes, as he once directed, with clarity and an unmistakably personal touch; he creates a Dietrich as romantic as any character she portrayed in his films. One can almost see the gauzes slide over the camera lens, the filtering and re-directing of lights. 'Despite her melancholy,' he writes of Dietrich in her pre-Hollywood days, 'she was well dressed and believed herself to be beautiful, although until this was radically altered by me, she had been photographed to look like a female impersonator. There are many unflattering photographs of her pre-*Blue Angel* period in existence, portraying an inhibited subject almost anxious to hide. Nevertheless, she distributed them to all

Opposite:
Sein grösster Bluff, with Harry Piel

11

and sundry with the air of bestowing a priceless gift . . .' He finishes with a slow close-up : 'Never before had I met so beautiful a woman who had been so thoroughly discounted and under-valued.'

At this remove, von Sternberg's view of Dietrich is ambivalent—but more seems to come from the heart than from the head.

Unquestionably, the Dietrich which was shaped by JVS and the demands of the depression public was a creature of dreams. She was his creation and bore as little resemblance to her former self as a fledgling to a bird of paradise. The earlier films amply prove it. However, it was Dietrich's decidedly German personality which filled out the phantoms of love which she embodied, giving them a dimension beyond von Sternberg's lights and instructions. She possessed a vital quality, that little 'extra something', which enabled her to survive and even flourish without JVS at the helm.

1929 Before Sternberg

Dishonoured 1931 The Sternberg touch

She was pretty in those days. Early photographs confirm her striking, if unformed, good looks. The tight curls on her large head, and the suggestive, monocled smile already hint at the fascinating ambiguity that was to become part of the legend. Yet there was no one before JVS capable of, or sufficiently interested in, releasing her face from its mask. Instead they pointed to her legs.

As her film work increased, however, discerning people began to notice something special. Reinhardt had already put her on the stage several times: one of her first performances was a small part in *The Taming of the Shrew* and soon after that she played Hippolyta in his *Midsummer Night's Dream*. That was in 1922, and by then she had made her film debut, probably in *So sind die Männer* (*That's What Men are Like*) although the film most often given as her first is Joe May's *Die Tragödie der Liebe* (1922) which starred Emil Jannings.

In 1926, after a period away from films for the birth of her daughter, Dietrich appeared in her first starring role on the stage in a popular revue called *Es Liegt in der Luft* (*It's In the Air*). She sang a duet with the aggressively masculine Marge Lion.

Wenn ein Weib den Weg verliert, with Willi Forst

Dietrich, delicate and soulful, made a marked contrast. Both women wore similar black dresses and large hats. The duet was called *Wenn die Liebe Freundin, mit der Lieben Freundin* (*When my Dear Friend with her Dear Friend*); each lady complemented the other's charms.

With that Dietrich had arrived. Reinhardt produced the American musical *Broadway* and she scored a notable success. At the last minute she was called upon to replace the star: asked if she could dance she showed that she could. Her career blossomed. She returned to Vienna, where, two years previously, she had played opposite Albert Basserman in *The Great Baritone*; this time it was for a musical comedy and a starring part in the film: *Wenn ein Weib den Weg verliert*, also known as *Café Electric*. In 1927, too, she made her first record, called *Peter* (Capitol T10282).

Marge Lion, Oskar Karlweis, and Dietrich in the revue **Es liegt in der Luft** 1926 (MFT 1126)

With Hedy Lamarr and Billy Wilder, on the set of **A Foreign Affair** 1948

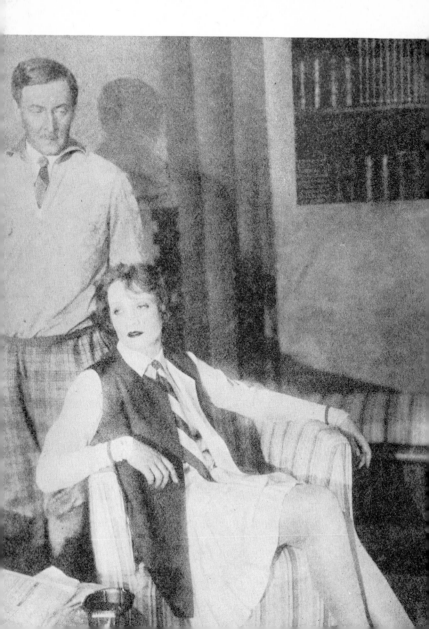

With Eric Odemar in Shaw's **Misalliance** 1928

Back in Berlin in 1928, she appeared in Shaw's *Misalliance*. Then she co-starred opposite Hans Albers (who also appeared in *Blue Angel*, and in Nazi films became the masculine symbol of all that was dear to the Aryan heart) in a satirical revue, *Zwei Krawatten*, in which Dietrich had a chance to speak a little English—a language with which she had been familiar since childhood. It was in this that von Sternberg, looking for a Lola for his *Blue Angel*, first saw her.

With Hans Albers in the revue **Zwei Krawatten** 1929

With Maurice Tourneur on set of **Das Schiff der Verlorenen Menschen**

Ich küsse ihre Hand, Madame, with Harry Liedtke

In 1929 she starred in no less than three films. In Maurice Tourneur's *Das Schiff der verlorenen Menschen* (*Ship of Lost Men*) she played Ethel, an intrepid ocean flyer. Kevin Brownlow found her 'remarkably beautiful, and very tomboyish'. He recalls a scene in which the crew are searching the ship for her: 'One man shines a torch into an apparently empty hole. Suddenly the torch lights up Marlene's feet. We tilt up and reveal her face, scared and pale in the torchlight. She does not look like Sternberg's "female impersonator". Yes, even without the other films, I would have taken notice of this pale, frightened, wide-eyed girl.' She also made *Die Frau nach der man sich sehnt* (*Three Loves*) and *Ich Küsse Ihre Hand, Madame*. Manfred Georg summed up her progress in films thus far: 'From that film on (*Die Frau nach der man sich sehnt*) and as a result of that film, her name was becoming known in film circles. It is difficult to forget the dramatic opening shots. A man and a woman see each other on a railway station. The romance of travel is in it. Suddenly,

Die Frau nach der man sich sehnt

a strange heart beats as one's own. Already one saw the large eyes of Dietrich; the smile which means so many things; the lure of the mouth and of the softly curling hair; one saw the wonder of a face, into which one tumbled; fell as into a bottomless well. Here was the lighting up of her personality, even if not yet the final breakthrough.'

Even without JVS Dietrich would, sooner or later, have become a success in German films. Everything pointed to it. Her stage training fitted her for sound, which was just coming in. But it is very doubtful whether she would have become a legend on her own.

More than thirty-five years later, when JVS records his first sight of Marlene Dietrich in the Berlin theatre, his feelings for her seep through: 'What little she had to do on that stage was not easily apparent; I remember only one line of dialogue. Here was the face I had sought, and, so far as I could tell, a figure that did justice to it. Moreover, there was something else I had not sought, something that told me that my search was over. She leaned against the wings with cold disdain for the buffoonery, in sharp contrast to the effervescence of the others. Here was not only a model who had been designed by Rops, but Toulouse-Lautrec would have turned a couple of handsprings had he laid eyes on her. Her appearance was ideal; what she did with it was something else again. That would be my concern.'

For her part she was uncertain. In an interview given to Ruth Biery (*Photoplay* 1933) she said candidly: 'I was not the big sensation in Europe that publicity stories have stated. Europe knows that. I was not very good in pictures. When he met me in Europe and asked me to make *Blue Angel* I said "You'd better not take me, I'm terrible in pictures".' Fortunately, JVS was a man who knew his own mind.

'I then put her into the crucible of my conception; blended her image to correspond with mine, and pouring lights on her until the alchemy was complete, proceeded with the test. She came to life and responded with an ease that I had never before encountered.'

The result was an unqualified success and a classic, which, when revived, decades later, still served as a yardstick. Based on Heinrich Mann's classic novel of bourgeois Germany, the story centred on the love of Professor Rath for the sexy singer, Lola Lola. For her he sacrifices his job, his self-respect, and his life.

Die Frau nach der man sich sehnt

'Overpage: 'Ich bin die fesche Lola' from **Der blaue Engel**

Professor Rath (Emile Jannings) the first time he sees . . .

The critics succumbed to the spell of Marlene much as Rath did to Lola Lola.

During the filming, Jannings realized that in Dietrich he had an unexpected rival. Apparently the rivalry between them was so strong that in one scene, in which he is supposed to strangle her, he took his part so seriously that his fingermarks could still be seen on her neck days later.

Dietrich was not present at the Berlin première. She was already on her way to America, having signed a contract with Paramount. UFA had delayed signing her, but, on von Sternberg's advice, Paramount did. After the showing of the film, a legend was born. The German film industry would try in vain to get her back.

Many of those who saw the film in April 1930, felt that it marked a renaissance of the German cinema. Though sound had been in use for about two years, most companies were still photographing stage plays and the camera's fluidity was undeveloped. Sternberg's use of sound in *The Blue Angel* was ahead of its time and realized its creative role in films. Though the photography and direction were widely praised and Jannings excelled in his role, the film's fame rests on the sensational emergence of Dietrich.

Siegfried Kracauer, writing in *From Caligari to Hitler*, saw her Lola Lola as 'a new incarnation of sex. This petty bourgeois Berlin tart, with her provocative legs and easy manners, showed an impassivity which incited one to grope for the secret behind her callous egoism and cool insolence. That such a secret existed was also intimated by her veiled voice, which, when she sang about her interest in love-making and nothing else, vibrated with nostalgic reminiscences and smouldering hopes.' A critic in the Berliner *Reichsfilmblatt*, April 1930, enthused: 'One is almost stunned by Marlene Dietrich's performance. Her ability to take over her scenes effortlessly, but with simple and total command is something we have until now never experienced.'

... Lola chanting her credo 'From Head to Foot I'm made for Love'

With Rosa Valetti in **Der Blaue Engel**

With Emil Jannings in **Der Blaue Engel**

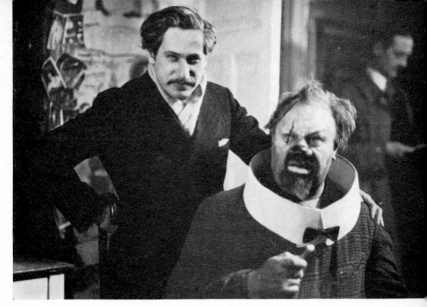

Josef von Sternberg with Jannings between scenes in **Der Blaue Engel**

With Hans Albers and Jannings in **Der Blaue Engel**

Berliner Borsenkurier, writing the day after the première, heralded 'The Sensation: Marlene Dietrich! She sings and plays almost without effort, phlegmatically. But this knowing phlegmaticism excites. She does not "act" common; she is. Her performance is all cinematic, nothing is theatrical.' When the film was re-issued in England in 1948, Dilys Powell wrote in her review: 'the photography, with its complex backgrounds of shifting lights and shadows, curtains and smoke and sordid fripperies, hints rather than states; and in the things half said, the picture half drawn, there is a strength which has been lost in the current cinema.'

For Gavin Lambert, writing in 1954, 'Dietrich's remote and fantastic creation'; and Sternberg's 'fastidious, perverse visual textured work', provided 'a work of art that is fascinating, narrow, unlikeable and, of course, flawlessly decadent'. In 1959 Edward Dmytrick re-made the film for Fox. It mis-mated Curt Jurgens in Jannings' role, and the Swedish Mai Britt as the immortal Lola Lola. Dietrich and JVS sued Fox but the case never came to court and was dropped.

'During the filming she complained that what I was instructing her to do would make it impossible for her ever to show her face again,' said JVS.

Opposite: **Der Blaue Engel**

The haunting last image

Though *The Blue Angel* marks the first time Sternberg worked with her, the evolution of Marlene Dietrich as the eternal feminine in a series of films that revealed the workings of destiny, began with *Morocco* (1930). One recalls the new Dietrich aboard a decrepit steamer docking in a foggy Moroccan seaport. The choice of place was purely poetic. As with all their films, set in Shanghai, Vienna, Paris, or turn-of-the century Seville, the location was selected for its romantic associations. From the first image to the by now classic finale, it was apparent that at long last Dietrich had found a director who knew how to tap her apparently inexhaustible ability for hard work, and enable her to arise phoenix-like on the screen, in a way which few others, before her or since, have approximated.

During the next five years (with one exception) she appeared only in von Sternberg films; six films that made a simple German Fräulein a part of modern mythology; six films whose greatness overshadowed much of both their subsequent work; six films so closely fitted to her new personality that they became, like the costumes she wore, an extension of herself. Yet no matter what role she played she was always recognizable as a passionate romantic, ready to sacrifice all for love.

In *Morocco*, as Amy Jolly, a cabaret entertainer, she sacrifices luxury and the adoration of Adolph Menjou, to follow legionnaire Cooper into the desert. She is oblivious to all else, still wearing a cocktail dress and high heels, which are hardly likely to afford any protection against the sand and the sun's heat.

In this moment all rationalization is swept away, the senses triumph over reason, we are drawn into a world where dreams are made reality by the revelation of Dietrich's still-deep beauty, and the visual genius of her director. (Dietrich was nominated for an Oscar.) In this world where love holds sway, secret dreams and hopes, illusions and facts hide under the same shadowed nettings.

Opposite : **Morocco** The dawn of a new face

Hand on hip, she dominated an era . . .
Left: **Morocco**   *Right:* **The Devil is a Woman**

Left: **The Scarlet Empress**
Right: At a party given by Marion Davis in 1935 she came as a swan

With Menjou, Ullrich Haupt, and Gary Cooper in **Morocco**

In later films the shadows were to beget more and more entwining shadows; the netting would be followed by veils and feathers, silk stockings, leather gloves, and furs. Streamers flutter and balloons soar. Shutters and venetian blinds cast shadowy bars to the heart, as inviolable as steel; the slow lap-dissolves, like heady liquors, dull our senses in a seductive wash of images at whose centre we find the *raison d'être*: Marlene Dietrich.

JVS on set of **Dishonored**, creating the world of illusion where reality and fantasy vie for the truth

Von Sternberg's poetic, chiaroscuric world met with success because it echoed the escapist desires of its public. The time was opportune. Sound, with *The Jazz Singer* (1928), had put an end to one of the film's most glorious romantic eras, at the apex of its artistic fulfilment. Von Sternberg's Dietrich-starred films provided a fitting epilogue to this era. The 'word', at first, made awful cinema, but it had some beneficial results. A new dimension demanded new faces, new directors. Few silent stars survived long, not even those whose voices were left untampered by enterprising studios. Important silent directors, whose demands had increased with their reputations, were now placed in cold storage by studio bosses who employed more pliable young men from the stage to direct the 'talkies'. Almost simultaneously, America, the land of milk and honey, found the ground lifted from beneath its feet as it plunged into the depression. Jazz babies and gay flappers had become grasping amoral 'golddiggers' by the time von Sternberg returned to America with his new discovery. *Our Modern Maidens* had become unwed mothers. The exciting, daring speakeasy, hangout for the hep youth of the twenties, was crowded from the nation's front pages by gloomy photos of soup-kitchens and long queues of the unemployed. The song of the time was no longer the chirpy, *Yes Sir, That's My Baby*, but the bitter lament *Remember My Forgotten Man*. The cinema provided the public with a welcome and inexpensive opiate. Exotic fantasy flourished, and nowhere more so than in von Sternberg's world, so divorced from the one they knew. A fog would lift, a lamp light, a veil slowly part, and there would be the guide through the labyrinth of a poet's musing.

It was a time of extremes and imagination, ranging from George Arliss's 'stagey' curios, to the lyrical heights of King Vidor's all-Negro musical *Hallelujah*. Film companies took risks because there was no longer any guarantee that the old formula story would still work. Mamoulian made *Love Me Tonight* and *Dr Jekyll and Mr Hyde*. Lubitsch produced his most sophisticated works like *Smiling Lieutenant* and *Trouble in Paradise*. Pirandello's *As You Desire Me* was adapted for the screen, Eugene O'Neill's six-hour stage play, *Strange Interlude*, saw the light of Hollywood. Universal made their horror classics and Warner Brothers took the lead with their musical extravaganzas like *42nd Street* and the *Golddigger* films. There was Garbo in the all-star *Grand Hotel*, there was Chaplin's *City Lights* and Lewis Milestone's anti-war classic, *All Quiet on The Western Front*. There was Mae West's

Ruby Keeler and fellow **Golddiggers of 1933**

Overpage: Dietrich in the desert of **Morocco**

JVS and Dietrich on set of **Morocco** with visitors Tertel and Clara Bow 1930

outrageously funny sex-farce *I'm No Angel* and, of course, the combined works of Dietrich and von Sternberg.

It was indeed a golden era. The virtually total freedom they commanded in the five years of their partnership was nothing less than spectacular, since studios were run rather like assembly lines.

Marlene's strong individuality and her enormous success with *Morocco*, *Dishonored*, and *Shanghai Express* enabled her to succeed in her own right, and not as another 'Garbo'. However, her close working relationship with von Sternberg took the place of the latter comparison and became a target for speculation. *Svengali*, the story of a hypnotist who exercises a strange power over his young protégée, had just come out, and it inspired rumours in the film world that von Sternberg had a similar hold over Dietrich. Why else, it was said, would this marvellous creature continue to work with one whom some thought of as a small, mannered, unbearable director.

Such a relationship was frequently denied by them, but as long as it sold tickets the studio was not adverse to fan articles devoted to it. Victor McLaglen, who co-starred in *Dishonored* (1931), was quoted: 'To look at those two gives me a temperature.' When von Sternberg's wife, Mrs Riza-Royce, took action against Marlene Dietrich for the alienation of her husband's affection to the tune of £100,000 and a further £20,000 for libel,

With JVS at the time of the lawsuit

the rumour-mongers felt justified in their continued insinuations. The studio urged her not to risk her career in a scandal but Dietrich denied the charges, contested them and won, since the writer of the article on which Mrs Riza-Royce had based her libel case admitted that it had all been his own, publicity-seeking fabrication. When Mrs Riza-Royce was interviewed years later for a series of reflections by the people who knew Marlene, her feelings on the matter were still warm. Having called Dietrich 'a blackspot' in her life, she gave an interesting appreciation of her former husband: 'Sternberg brought out the best in her.' Interspersing her re-collections with some strongly worded personal opinions of Dietrich, she then continued:

'Before he worked with her, his films were presented with the legend "A Josef von Sternberg production". After he was in Marlene's hooks, his films advertised Marlene Dietrich in big letters, and his name was small and insignificant underneath.

'Before Marlene, he was known as a director who could turn out a film in 24 days. He never shot a scene more than twice. But when he started to work with Marlene, he would shoot a scene 20 or 60 times. That's why his films began to cost a fortune.'

Since studios indirectly controlled fan magazines in those days, it remains a mystery why Paramount allowed one of their most successful directors to be made a laughing stock in articles which pictured him as a mustachioed bogeyman with a riding crop who directed a glamorous disciple. It may have been that von Sternberg was too aloof to submit to the dictates of the men who controlled the purse strings. He made the films he wanted to make, as he wanted to, and seemed quite unconcerned at the intrigues and animosity which this total disregard for studio politics provoked. While the films made money this was overlooked and praise was lavish.

Not unreasonably, studios wanted their stars to make three or four quick films a year, for fast returns, instead of one that took months, no matter how superb it might be. Von Sternberg preferred to take his time and Dietrich steadfastly refused to work with any other director. At the first hint of a drop in the box-office of their films there were renewed attempts to split the team. Dietrich adamantly informed Paramount's production head, B. P. Schulberg, that she would 'never make pictures in America with anyone but Mr von Sternberg'. This statement was met with rift-insinuations in the magazines.

MARLENE DIETRICH
"**THE DEVIL IS A WOMAN**"
LIONEL ATWILL · CESAR ROMERO
A Paramount Picture directed by JOSEF VON STERNBERG

A typical poster for one of their films

In an interview she gave in January 1933, Dietrich explained why, following rows with the studio, she was leaving for a long holiday in Europe: 'Mr von Sternberg is tired of pictures. He wants to go to Japan. . . . I wanted to be free, when he was free. I, myself, don't like making pictures. I can live without them. I haven't got to act to be happy. I am happy with Mr von Sternberg because I trust him. How do I know what another director could do with me?' She added that she worked when von Sternberg asked her to, simply because she knew what he could do for her and with her, 'not because of any Svengali and Trilby influence. I am devoted to him, but I made the devotion myself because my brain told me to. If you meet a great person you become devoted. He has no patience with stupid people. He has no patience with me while I am stupid. Which I understand. Why should he waste his time.' It was not the first time that her indifference to film work forced the studio to promise her the moon, or its earthly equivalent—von Sternberg to direct her films. First she went on her European holiday, and made front page headlines around the world when 'sophisticated' Paris reacted with shock and boos to the sight of Dietrich, togged in a man's suit and beret, with matching ensemble for her little daughter, strolling casually along the Champs-Elysées. She had stated publicly why she would work only with JVS, yet this was ignored and it was still taken for granted that von Sternberg had persuaded her to remain detached from 'the crowd' as he himself had always done. In 1933, on one of the rare occasions when von Sternberg revealed his feelings to the press, he said: 'It's a matter of absolute indifference to me whether I am praised or censured.'

Paramount released *The Blue Angel* after Dietrich's success in America had been established with *Morocco*. The fact that *The Blue Angel*, though a sensation on the Continent, was far from attaining the same popularity as *Morocco* in America served only to emphasize the public's preference for Dietrich's many-sided illusory woman of the world to her superb bourgeois vamp Lola Lola. Although von Sternberg's work evolved according to a private logic, the subsequent development of their films (which gave maximum exposure as actress and personality to Dietrich) was based on his realization that in Dietrich he had one of those rare beings who could be made to give substance to dreams without losing any of their elusive fragility.

Her preference for trousers made headlines and fashions—with husband
Rudolf Sieber arriving in Paris 1932

Dietrich's similarity to . . .

In the spring of 1931 there was nothing but acclaim for his direction of the sensational German import. When magazines asked their readers to select the 'exotic of the exotics', the choice quickly narrowed to Dietrich and Garbo. Except for the temporary threat of Tallulah Bankhead, they were never to have any other serious competition. Film-goers split down the middle in advancing the praise of their favourite. At the height of the debate, one excited fan wrote: 'Why bring in a terrible foreign production like *Blue Angel* with Marlene Dietrich? We shout loud and fierce. "Send her back!".'

... Garbo was not accidental 1931

Appeal to the female public cannot be ignored in the creation of a sex symbol. Aware of this, JVS, provocatively, but with great taste, used sequences of Dietrich wearing a man's tailored evening dress, (*Morocco, Blonde Venus*); disguised as a pilot (*Dishonored*) and as the inspired leader of the Russian cavalry (*Scarlet Empress*). Women admired her as strongly as did the men. One wrote in: 'Dietrich is a flaming sunset!' Another declared: 'Marlene Dietrich has everything that Garbo has and something else besides—humor!'

49

Having her wear trousers was not meant to stimulate a fashion which not long after the film was shown encouraged women to ignore skirts in favor of the less picturesque lower half of male attire.'—JVS, *Fun in a Chinese Laundry*

Left: **Dishonored**   *Right:* **Morocco**

Blonde Venus

Amy Jolly meets legionnaire Tom Brown (Gary Cooper) in **Morocco**

Garbo had long been JVS's ideal incarnation of the magic of female glamour, consequently he often photographed Dietrich from 'garboesque' angles. But he felt that 'glamour' could not be created by the woman, no matter how desirable, it was the work of a craftsman, the director. He defined it as, 'the result of the dark-light in colours, the play of the lights on the landscape of the face, the use of the background through the composition, through the aura of the hair; and by casting mysterious shadows into the eyes'.

JVS was not adverse to giving Dietrich considerable credit for their films. Speaking to Ruth Biery in October 1931, he is quoted as saying: 'I think I will get sick on this next picture (*Shanghai Express*) and stay away and let her direct. She almost directed *Morocco* and *Dishonored*.' When Miss Biery, an astute reporter, seemed incredulous, JVS insisted: 'No, I mean it! The entire stage scene in *Morocco* was her idea. The songs were hers and it was the best scene in the picture.'

Recently he denied having said this, but admitted that *Morocco* was the direct result of Dietrich's having presented him with a copy of the book *Amy Jolly* by Benno Vigny to read on his trip back to America. He then added, 'Well, she's an extraordinary woman. She was a great beauty and she was a fine asset. She responded beautifully. She gave me an image; not exactly what I wanted—sometimes better than what I wanted. She was quite a gal!'

In 1932 he made *Shanghai Express*. It was to be their biggest commercial success, grossing some three million dollars when the value of the dollar was five times that of today, and admission prices were still 10c (1s) as compared to today's $1 (7s) plus. In many ways it was the apotheosis of their work. The plot, again scripted by Jules Furthman, lyrically captured the hypnotism of the enchanted lovers. Set in exotic China, aboard a train carrying prostitutes, dope peddlars, missionaries, and Chinese war lords, it was a love story in the tradition of German folklore. Estranged lovers, Clive Brook and Dietrich had to overcome three tests of faith, in order to live happily ever after. In the first few masterful shots, von Sternberg evokes the background against which the story is to be played.

As Shanghai Lily in **Shanghai Express**
Overpage: Capt. Harvey (Clive Brook) meets his old flame Shanghai Lily

Shanghai Express

Peking: the railway station—exciting expectancy—the anonymous cosmopolitan crowds—the noise and chaos of the Far East. Captain Donald Harvey a stiff-backed English officer, calm in the sea of confusion surrounding him, waits for his train to leave. The wheels churn slowly—aboard the train he stands in the corridor looking out at the station—steam momentarily blurs our vision—it clears—he turns—we see the Princess of the fairy tale—Dietrich.

Disguised in the traditional garb of the glamorous tramps of the East, with sleek black feathers, a symbol of evil or a sign of enchantment: the Black Swan. Her face is shadowed, only the wonderful mouth shows beneath the netted veiling.

As with all their films, von Sternberg, *writing with the camera*, creates in Dietrich another Anna Karenina, another Mme Bovary. His emotional needs seem to be focused through the eye of the camera which becomes almost 'voyeuristic' in the way it sees women as supreme glories, even in unspeakably sordid backgrounds. The actual content of the dialogue does not interest him, but its sounds do. He uses silences to reveal more intimate facets of his characters. When the camera takes over the script, JVS has no peer.

Dietrich is the prism through which love's white light is analysed into the spectrum and von Sternberg is a modern Symbolist. Romance breathes from the furs softening her shoulders, the wild scent of her leather gloves, and the rasping sensuous grit of her veils; from the poetic heights of her moon-bathed blondness, to the sexual immediacy of her lover's cap, tilted rakishly over her forehead. The dialogue becomes the high-wire on which the hero must balance while demonstrating his faith for years before his complete acceptance of the spoken word had resulted in his losing the woman he loved. The ground Captain Harvey treads in the Shanghai Express is steeped with danger; words are to be misunderstood, eyes tricked by shadows. Harvey first sees her as she once was, Madeleine, then as she now appears to be, gowned as a lush whore, Shanghai Lily. Part of the initial exchange of dialogue is here given in a written approximation of its hypnotic rhythm, paralleling the monotone of the train, the sentences broken with apparently irrelevant pauses.

With Clive Brook aboard the Shanghai Express

With a rare grasp of metrical music in English, the background is filled in, feelings clarified, and the tests begin.

SL : Have I lost my looks?
H : No. . . . You're more beautiful than ever
SL : How have I changed?
H : You know. . . .
    I wish I could describe it
SL : Welllll Docccc
    I've changed my name
H : Married?
SL : (*a spoken slow laugh*) No. . . .
    It took more than one man
    to change my name to (*pause for a count of five while lights make patterns with the black veil on her face*)
    Shanghai Lily. . . .
H : So you're Shanghai Lily!
SL : The notorious
    White Flower
             of China
    You've heard of me
    and you always
    believed
    what you heard

Moments later, back in his compartment, Harvey quells the ranting of a missionary, who objects to the presence of Shanghai Lily aboard the train, with a cutting: 'See here, Sir. She's a friend of mine.' Under the disapproving gaze of his fellow travellers he escorts her to dinner.

Almost all the other travellers, like Shanghai Lily, are in some form of disguise. The grouchy hypochondriac 'importer' is really a dope smuggler; the missionary Mr Carmichael initially appears to be against Shanghai Lily, yet it is he who later tells Harvey that he should reason with his heart and not as a 'man of science'. The half-caste proves to be a Chinese war lord, and the enigmatic Hui Fei, apparently another prostitute, plays the part of Shanghai Lily's guardian angel. The vital test begins when the Chinese war lord holds the train to ransom and intends to blind Captain Harvey for assaulting him. Shanghai Lily offers to stay as Chang's mistress, if he will allow Harvey to go unharmed. Hui Fei kills Chang and helps Shanghai Lily back on to the train.

A bandits' hideout or an enchanted castle, a maze of lattices, shadows and half lights.
Henry Chang (Warner Oland), Shanghai Lily, and Major Lenard (Emile Chautard)

Harvey, unaware of the reason for her decision, thought that she was voluntarily staying behind with a rich lover. The last part of the journey is taken up with his private torment, paralleled by her agony as she waits for the last and greatest proof of his love. Alone she prays, and her metaphoric disguises fall from her until she is revealed as the first woman and the madonna. Never again was one to see such tender alchemy as resulted from an inspired Sternberg and his inspiration, Dietrich. Love triumphs. Love in all its facets constitutes Sternberg's world of illusion-flecked truths. *Shanghai Express* is one of those rare instances when an artist reveals his own aesthetic philosophy.

Up to and including *Shanghai Express* Dietrich had been the passive object acted upon by the forces of her love. *Blonde Venus* forms the cinematic bridge that she crosses to become the active force. Released at the end of 1932, this film has several autobiographical undertones, echoing the supposed real-life relationship between director and star that occupied the press at the time. It was Jules Furthman's last script for JVS; Richard Wallace had been set to direct, but Dietrich's refusal to work with another director placed Paramount in the position of having to accept JVS. Like most of their films, it was based on an *'original'* story by him. This time he adds another dimension to Dietrich, illuminating her as a wife and mother. Her femininity is enriched as we see her bathing her young son, tucking him into bed and

Opposite: **Shanghai Express**
With Dickie Moore in **Blonde Venus**

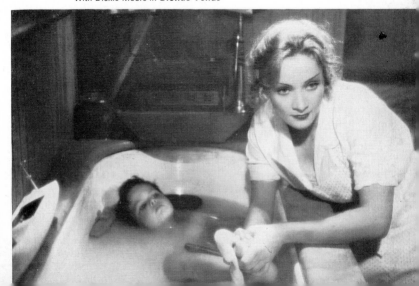

The 'Blonde Venus' after shedding gorilla skin

singing him to sleep. She is Helen Faraday, formerly a German cabaret artist, now happily married to Herbert Marshall, an American research scientist who contracts a dangerous illness. The only doctor who can save his life is in Germany. As they are unable to afford the treatment his wife decides to walk the well-worn street of sin. Along the way she works in a nightclub; billed as the 'Blonde Venus' she has a particularly effective sequence that has become a high watermark in the camp mythology of Marlene. It is the 'Hot Voodoo' number. A chain of hip-swinging, lithe negresses undulate on to the night-club floor, trailing behind them a monstrous gorilla who makes threatening sweeps at the audience. Then, swaying alone at the centre of the stage, the gorilla, its belly cradled in its huge arms, suddenly removes one paw, then the other, then the frightening head. From the hairy ugliness of the skin steps the new-born Blonde Venus.

Fleeing dingy hotel with Dickie Moore, **Blonde Venus**

Finding refuge in a hay cart, **Blonde Venus**

With unsuspecting detective (Sidney Toler), **Blonde Venus**

The husband, back home, learns by chance how his wife earned the money to pay for his cure. Forced to choose between a life of luxury with her lover (Cary Grant in an early role) and her adored son, she flees with the boy, to be hounded by an embittered husband and the police. In swift, concise, dramatic images, which refute the criticisms of 'still-life' photography often levelled at his films, Sternberg depicts the depths to which she must sink to keep her son. The hotel rooms deteriorate: the cities become one-horse hamlets, even the back of a hay cart serves as a temporary idyllic refuge. She finds herself in day court, having solicited to earn the money to feed her son, and at last hits rock bottom in a flora-fauna brothel in the deep south. Forced to accept the fact that she cannot keep the boy in this milieu, she hands him over to the policeman who has been trailing her.

As the train bearing her child pulls out of the station, a tragic nobility enshrines her, a windswept newspaper clings to her legs, her straw hat rains shadowy bars across her face.

After a spell in her private inferno, during which she is the white-tuxedoed sensation of European nightclubs, Grant finds her in Paris and takes her back to her husband, who forgives her at their child's bedside.

With husband Ned Faraday (Herbert Marshall), **Blonde Venus**

With daughter, husband, and JVS 1931–2

While the film never meant much to either of them, or so one gathers from Sternberg's autobiography, one does not have to look far beneath the surface to find in it an indirect reply by JVS to the gossips and rumour-mongers. Neither a glamorous career as the fabulous Blonde Venus (Dietrich's sensational success in Hollywood) nor a rich lover who could offer her everything (presumably director JVS who also first saw her in a cabaret and brought her to Hollywood), could compete in Helen Faraday's heart with her love for home and child (Dietrich's well-known love of her daughter Maria, and of her husband Rudolf Sieber, who jointed her shortly after her arrival in Hollywood).

In 1933, on Paramount's insistence and with the approval of JVS, Dietrich made *Song of Songs* for Mamoulian. She was Lily Czepanek, a peasant girl, who becomes in turn a sculptor's model, a lady of society, and a café singer. The film was a moderate success and is best remembered for a nude statue of the star that figures in it. It was apparent on the set that Dietrich was unhappy working with someone else and before each scene, the story went, she would walk up to the mike and whisper, 'Joe, where are you?' It must have been rather unsettling for Mamoulian.

With sculptor Brian Aherne in **Song of Songs**

With Victor McLaglen in **Dishonored**

Overpage:
Shanghai Express

By now, niggardly criticisms, which had begun after *Dishonored*,
were to turn into a tide of public apathy and critical resentment
against any film which Dietrich was to make with JVS. Leonard
Hall, having seen *Dishonored*, wrote of Dietrich, then in her
meteoric rise to stardom, 'Owing to the mistaken generosity and
zeal of the talented Herr Direktor, they (her legs) constitute an
overdose of sex appeal, a plethora of beauty and a definite menace
to the future sound and solid career of the Belle of Berlin, for a
time I didn't know if I was looking at a spy drama or a hosiery
show !' Dietrich, as Austrian spy X 27, was seen piloting a plane
behind enemy lines ; exchanging kisses for secrets ; disguised as a

Above and opposite:
Showing the versatility of Magda, secret agent X 27 in **Dishonored**

dim-witted kitchen maid; going to her ignoble death with a last smile to a heartbroken lieutenant who cannot give the order for the execution; Dietrich as a streetwalker, and a martyr for love; each aspect added another dimension to the growing myth. As Raymond Durgnat realized, 'the plot logic of *Dishonored* exists in order that the visuals may drift into scenes as self-justifying as the sonnets of Mallarmé.' *Picture Play* led popular opinion in their review: 'How much of her defiance as a streetwalker, her terrible charm as the secret service decoy, her gaiety and abandon in the Russian peasant disguise is due to brilliant direction and how much to Dietrich's acting ability is unimportant. She is unique.' Today it may be difficult to understand how in less than three years popular opinion turned against their films.

With Lew Cody in **Dishonored**

With Victor McLaglen in **Dishonored**

Dietrich may have made few films, but whenever films were mentioned, her name would come up. Nothing she did failed to reach the public. But, unless fostered with variety, public adulation is eventually bound to wane, and although, like Garbo, her appeal on the Continent was still so strong that she was in no real danger, the storm warnings were up in America.

Yet her personal stock stayed high, she became the darling of the intelligentsia and the classy little magazines. Though good for the ego, it meant nothing at the box-office and its overall effect was usually adverse.

But it was not because of Dietrich's talents and range as an actress that she became a legend. She did so as one of the rare successful personifications of Love's envoy. Few of his fellow directors or his critics understood how JVS achieved the astonishing transformation in the personality of any woman who passed before his lens and few of her subsequent American directors were any better at bringing out Dietrich's hypnotic personality as revealed by JVS than their German counterparts had been. One of the few to appreciate his ability was the former silent screen star, Louise Brooks, who is as shrewdly perceptive about films as she was beautiful in them : 'Dietrich always mystified me because I wondered "What in hell is she thinking about—with that long, gorgeous stare ?" Sternberg solves the mystery in one simple line of direction. He used to say to her "Count six and look at the lamp-post as if you couldn't live without it !" So, by giving her these strange thoughts to concentrate on, to build her mind, he also of course gave her this strange, alien mystery. She never had it with any other director. . . . He could direct every woman he touched. He could make her lovely ! He could take the most gauche, awkward specimen, and turn her into a *dynamo* of sex ! . . . Sternberg could look at a woman and say, "This is beautiful about her, I'll leave it, not change it. And this is ugly about her. I'll eliminate it. Not change her, but take away the bad and leave what is beautiful so she is complete."

'For instance, Dietrich—if you ever saw her in those pre-von Sternberg films, she was just . . . dynamic ! Full of energy and awkward. Just dreadful ! . . . So he simply cut out her movements and painted her on the screen in beautiful striking poses, staring at a lamp-post.'

Opposite: **Shanghai Express**, off set

The Sternberg touch times seven

Opposite, top left:
Hedy Lamarr in **I Take this Woman** 1940

top right:
Akemi Negishi in **The Saga of Anatahan** 1953

bottom left:
Esther Ralston in **The Case of Lena Smith** 1929

bottom right:
Evelyn Brent in **The Last Command** 1928

Above:
Gene Tierney and Ona Munson in
The Shanghai Gesture 1941

right:
Anna May Wong in **Shanghai Express** 1932

Von Sternberg's strength as a director and his control over the actors were partly the result of the emotional reaction that he provoked in the people he worked with. They resented his autocratic manner but usually gave their best in an attempt to penetrate his aura of detachment. With Dietrich he lost this detachment. In *Fun in a Chinese Laundry* he gives fascinating glimpses into the creative process of an artist. Yet the only clue he provides to his working relationship with Marlene Dietrich, and to why he continued working with her for five years, is in the Paul Gauguin quote which prefaces his chapter about her: 'When extreme sentiments blend in the deep of a person, when they burst out, and when the entire mind flows like lava from a volcano—the cold calculations of reason have not presided over this emission, and who knows when and where the work started?'

It is necessary in writing about Marlene Dietrich the actress to deal at some length with the man responsible for shaping the myth. To observe the Dietrich of those films, idolize her, but relegate the films themselves to the land of camp seems, in my opinion, to lack perception. For many, the pinnacle of their work together was unquestionably *The Scarlet Empress*. It was made after von Sternberg's return from the Orient, and an eastern sense of hedonism prevails in the film, with Dietrich as the fabulous, frenzied 'happening' of a rampant libido. It was released in 1934; the depression had ended. With the returning security came conformity, followed by censorship. *The Scarlet Empress* was an attack on all the prurient; it was thirty years ahead of its time, and suffered for it. Every celluloid inch of this masterpiece marked it as a stone of the first water, enhanced by the superlative performance of the star.

It is about the marriage of the innocent young Sophia Frederica to the Grand Duke Peter of Russia, and the insurrection which led to her becoming the new Empress Catherine. Around this von Sternberg built up a series of shock impacts that impinge on the subconscious. Few things are as unsettling as seeing a character about whom we have certain preconceived ideas behaving contrary to type. Did any Empress ever act quite so randily as the old Empress Elizabeth from the first moment we see her? She is resplendent in robes of State, courtiers shuffle in subjugated silence, the huge stone eagle over the throne, with spread wings and malevolent eyes, dominates the magnificent room, an aura of barbaric majesty clings to everything. Suddenly, with total disregard for her personal majesty and the reaction of her

With Olive Tell, John Lodge, and Louise Dresser in **The Scarlet Empress**

guests, the Empress addresses the virile officer who has escorted the naïve sixteen-year old Catherine through Russia; she pulls him towards her and kisses him passionately. The unexpected becomes the norm. Claude-Jean Philippe exulted: 'The close-up of the characters concentrates our waiting, prolongs the mystery. These faces, degraded or exalted by some elemental passion, which is all on the surface, suddenly seem to us to reveal the most secret and profound of secrets. The veil of interior life is slowly raised. When Marlene chews a piece of straw with that royal insolence which we know is hers; when her breath makes a candle flame flicker, we are on the brink of the unexplainable.' This phantasmagoria sweeps us to the heights of madness.

The young Catherine . . .

With John Lodge in **The Scarlet Empress**
. . . has learnt the value of her sex.

The young Catherine quickly learns the value of her sexual powers as a means of self-preservation at the barbaric Russian Court where sexuality is synonymous with power, and power is Trumps. In the magnificent finale, amid the deafening peal of bells and the tumultuous surging of the crowd, Catherine gallops up the Palace steps at the head of her Imperial Cavalry. She is totally depraved. Her eyes stare insanely from their cavernous sockets, her brows are arched to their sensuous extremes, and her cheeks sink into her face in a delirious contraction of hedonistic excitement released by the narcotic of Absolute Power, as she stands by the coveted throne.

Von Sternberg wrote the screen play and selected the statuary, and ikons (specially designed by Peter Ballbusch and Richard Kollorsz) as well as the music, which he conducted.

In *The Devil is a Woman*, Concha cynically remarks that 'critics never value genius', possibly reflecting JVS's reaction to the critical reception of *Scarlet Empress*. The public avoided it; almost to a man the critics dismissed it. Those who saw its merits were in a minority. The most intelligent and perceptive review was that of an anonymous *Times* critic '. . . the subject of the film is not Catherine, nor a particular episode in history, but the Russia of the past, seen in a fantastically distorting mirror, extravagantly oriental, infinitely sinister, holy and horrible.

'Almost every effect is got by the scenery and settings. Human beings are continuously mixed up with the statuary, which seems more alive than they . . . the director has exercised an extraordinary ingenuity in the invention of ever more appalling still-life, until, in the end, the mere murder of the Tsar is as nothing beside the cakestand on his dinner table, fashioned in the shape of skeletons.'

Miss Lejeune, in the *Observer*, led the negative majority with a review that might have originated in Victorian England. Outraged that the old Empress, magnificently played by Louise Dresser, was not her idea of an Empress, she then compared Dietrich's performance with Elizabeth Bergner's interpretation of the role in Korda's production released the same year: 'Miss Bergner's attack on the part may actually—and does—get nearer the real Empress than Miss Dietrich's reading, which suggests a lady with a good pair of legs and few other resources at all.' She found the film 'ill-mannered' and lecherous—even the original sets failed to please her.

Another critic quoted the expenditure of 'a sum in the region of a quarter of a million pounds sterling in evolving such a film nightmare . . .'. Von Sterberg could have made a laughing stock of critics and of Ernst Lubitsch, then Paramount's production head, who had accused him of squandering money on a short crowd sequence. In reality this had cost virtually nothing, since JVS had lifted it from Lubitsch's silent film *The Patriot*, and re-worked it here for the powerful climactic effect.

Dietrich's performance, always underrated, was a rare accomplishment. At the time she was nearly thirty-four, yet the transition from a bewildered sixteen-year-old to a highly intelligent sexual despot of nineteen was an achievement few actresses could boast. Perhaps her future employers agreed with Miss Bergner when she said, 'If I had her beauty, I wouldn't need to act!' for they never again gave her such an opportunity.

Overpage: **The Devil is a Woman** with Cesar Romero

The Scarlet Empress and supporters

With Don Pasqual (Lionel Atwill) in **The Devil is a Woman**

Sternberg has said of their last film together: 'With the dice loaded so that I could not win, I paid a final tribute to the lady I had seen leaning against the wings of a Berlin stage. . . .' It was to be called *Caprice Espagnol*, but Lubitsch changed it to *The Devil is a Woman*—a more commercial title. The woman was Dietrich: Hollywood jokesters cast von Sternberg as the devil. Concha, a siren of turn-of-the-century Seville, entices men to their ruin in a story with strong sado-masochistic undertones. It was impossible in this seductive creature of lace and veils to recognize the once plump German Fraulein whom few had found photogenic. It had long been implied, without any factual justification, that the screen relationship of Dietrich and her male co-stars was a reflection of her working relationship with her director. In this film, both Lionel Atwill and Cesar Romero bore an undeniable resemblance to von Sternberg at that time. (Years later Jacques Demy adopted von Sternberg's idea of different actors portraying the same character at different ages in his film *Lola*, which he dedicated to Dietrich.)

During the shooting, von Sternberg announced to the press: 'Fräulein Dietrich and I have progressed as far as possible together. My being with Dietrich any further will not help her or me. If we continue we would get into a pattern which would be harmful to both of us.' Dietrich, apparently unaware of this decision, was hurt and upset and refused to speak to him for several days.

Concha Perez is the only woman Dietrich played, who, without any logical motivation, takes pleasure in the wanton destruction of the male. Even Catherine's despotism was caused by severe traumatic shocks. Concha casually tells one of her admirers: 'I came to see if you were dead. If you loved me enough, you would have killed yourself.'

Dietrich's reputation as a *femme fatale* rests on two films: *The Blue Angel* and this one. In most of her films she suffered more in the cause of love than did the men. For a *femme fatale* that's not a good record. But she more than makes up for it with *The Devil is a Woman* (based on *The Woman and the Puppet* by Pierre Louys). Her Concha is Galatea before she becomes flesh and blood; one feels that her hopeful Pygmalion has finally become resigned to it. Resignation is a form of death, and Henri Agel spoke of von Sternberg's 'suicidal lyricism'. Certainly the film is a triumph of the director's visual style. Discussing this, as

The Devil is a Woman

The Devil is a Woman

observed in Dietrich's incendiary beauty, *Variety* (1935) wrote:
'Not even Garbo in the Orient has approached, for spectacular
effects, Dietrich in Spain. With fringe, lace, sequins, carnations,
chenille, nets, embroideries, and shawls, Miss Dietrich is hung,
wrapped, draped, swathed and festooned . . . Miss Dietrich
emerges . . . as a glorious achievement, a supreme consolidation of
the sartorial, make-up, and photographic arts.'

The film completes Sternberg's fascinated search for the faces of
Love. Sex without love becomes an inextinguishable lust that can
only be sated by Death. Another cinematic poet, Cocteau, also
envisioned the artist's death 'masquerading as a woman', in
Orphée. There Death could be conquered by a 'great labour of
Love' and it was Death's minion who helped the poet escape from
the Underworld. In *The Devil is a Woman*, Death wins, by tricking
Love to gain its end. In the guise of an irresistible seductress,
Concha–Death–Devil, leaves the virile young man (Romero) to
return to her older lover (Atwill) who is mortally wounded—not
to save him, but to make sure that he does not recover. She appears
at the hospital clad in funereal black.

The Devil is a Woman

O. O. Green, in his review, felt: 'The very sharp edge of Sternberg's Marlene is Sternberg rather than Marlene, for in a sense she is his feminine mirror.' Sternberg himself pointed this out to his *Cahiers du Cinéma* interviewers in 1965: 'You must understand that in my films Marlene is not herself. Remember that. Marlene is not Marlene. I am Marlene, she knows that better than anyone.' Dietrich, the actress, plays the part, of the remote temptress who here represents Sternberg's conception. Sternberg's dream is Concha, the unattainable ideal (Dietrich), but is he not also Pasqualito (Lionel Atwill), the dreamer who falls in love with the romantic illusion and is consumed and destroyed by it? Or, as Fritz Lang once said, 'Von Sternberg created a person, and then that person destroyed the creator.' It seems perverse that both von Sternberg and Dietrich should select this particular film as one of their favourites.

The cycle was complete. Dietrich was again on her own. The rise of Lola Lola and the fall of Professor Immanuel Rath had found its real-life parallel in Dietrich's ascent to stardom, and the slow eclipse of von Sternberg's career as a director.

Her beauty, like a barometer, reflected the ardour of her lovers.

Above and opposite: **The Devil is a Woman**

It's often said that imitation is the highest form of flattery, but it only takes, repeats, and destroys.

The results of the combination of Dietrich and Sternberg were praised and admired until his techniques and her make-up had been carefully studied by other studios. As soon as box-office returns showed that Paramount had a winner to help stave off the effects of the depression (and it was well known at the time that *Morocco* saved Paramount from near collapse) the market was flooded with cheaply-made imitation 'Sternbergs'.

Prior to the advent of Dietrich, studios had been scrambling for a Garbo in their backlot. Now they wanted a Dietrich as well. Browless, languid, chain-smoking creatures poured into Hollywood from every corner of the globe. If they weren't born with a foreign accent they quickly acquired one. They appeared through screens of cigarette smoke, and vanished into them as quickly as they arrived. Some made it, but they were few and short-lived, adding their eyebrows to the shavings on the barber's-shop floor, and sketching in new antennae as wispy as their fabricated backgrounds.

Hollywood talent scouts rummaged through Europe, returning with waves of exotics in their tow. In the search for substitutes many talented actresses were sacrificed. Great continental favourites were brought to Hollywood, but usually the films they made there were far from successful and the clever ones soon returned to their own countries.

Garbo had an individuality which few of her fellow actresses wanted to emulate, since it was partly founded on her renunciation of what many were longing for—publicity. When Garbo renounced it, she was already established. In Dietrich's case it seemed easier. Few could really match the style with which she sported her trouser suits, and no one ever 'wore' a cigarette between her fingers in quite the same erotic way. None achieved her screen presence as von Sternberg displayed it though they copied her make-up and demanded the best soft focus lenses to be had. Future stars, such as Carole Lombard, went through their 'Dietrich phase' and few of the Paramount starlets were immune to the spell of her beauty.

Circa 1935

Paramount seem to have been unwilling or unable to see that Dietrich's ability to triumph over naïve scripts was as unique as Garbo's, and, anxious to repeat a successful formula, they quickly signed up Isa Miranda when Dietrich left them. Not only did this beautiful Italian star look like Dietrich, she starred in *Hotel Imperial*, originally planned as *I Love a Soldier*, a vehicle for Dietrich.

Rare still from unmade film **I Loved a Soldier** 1936

Isa Miranda

Top left: Anna Sten

top right: Brigitte Helm

bottom left: Dietrich

Right: Gwili Andre

below: Carole Lombard

George Bancroft and Evelyn Brent in **Underworld** 1927

At the height of the vogue, most studios had Dietrich imitations on their payroll. Tala Birell was a much heralded exotic of the time. RKO produced Gwili Andrée, a beautiful model from Denmark. Samuel Goldwyn advertised the fact that he spent a million dollars on his import in the exotic sweepstakes, the beautiful Russian actress Anna Sten. In Germany there was Brigitte Helm, the original choice for *Blue Angel*, and the Swedish actress Zarah Leander. Eventually the best imitation of Dietrich became Dietrich herself, an embodiment of the legendary glamour that was hers.

Paul Muni and Ann Dvorak in **Scarface** 1932

Overpage:
Taking a bath in **Knight without Armor**

Her humour, warmth and intelligence saved her from becoming
the caricature that is so often the fate of surviving legends.

Almost from the outset, von Sternberg's films influenced other
Hollywood directors, particularly Howard Hawks, whose gangster
film, *Scarface*, owes much to *Underworld*, sometimes even complete camera set-ups. Hawks often worked with script writers
who had previously worked with Sternberg. Ben Hecht who
worked on *Underworld* also wrote *Scarface*, and Jules Furthman
who wrote *To Have and Have Not* and *Rio Bravo* for Hawks.

Barbara Stanwyck in **Double Indemnity** 1944

Hawks successfully adapted Sternberg's approach to the feminine mystique, bringing Sternberg's women down to earth in a man's world, 'blowing up' what JVS saw through a microscope. Few of the Sternberg follow-ups stand on their own today; Frank Capra's *The Bitter Tea of General Yen* proves an exception. Barbara Stanwyck, who is to Dietrich as Hawks is to Sternberg,

Manpower 1941

(as Billy Wilder recognized in casting her as Lola Dietrichson in *Double Indemnity*), gave a superb performance with Nils Asther in a love story of East and West, inspired by *Shanghai Express*.

But in the immediate post-depression era there was no room for non-conformists and JVS left Paramount, with his last two films as flops behind him.

Lubitsch, then Paramount Production Head, personally supervised the production of Dietrich's first film without von Sternberg, and ace director Frank Borzage was assigned to show how much more could be done with her.

The film *Desire* (1936) was a remake of the German film *Die schönen Tage in Aranjuez*, starring Brigitte Helm (1933). Cooper was given the best reviews and Dietrich, who had arrived on the set with JVS as her personal camera advisor, was said to be very much in the Sternberg mould. C. A. Lejeune now noticed a 'human quality added to her glamour, and a delicious sense of comedy to her sex appeal'. After appearing in two films for other studios, she returned to make *Angel* (1937) directed by Lubitsch, who found her pleasant to work with and able to 'take direction intelligently and without resentment'.

Left:
With Mae West and director Raoul Walsh on the set of **Klondike Annie** 1936

Desire

With Charles Boyer in **The Garden of Allah**

Dietrich gave a polished, subtly-blended comedy performance as the flirtatious wife of an English diplomat (Herbert Marshall). But this did not save the film which Basil Wright, in *The Spectator*, found 'insufferably dull in part', although Marlene, 'whose film it presumably is, looks happier, acts better, and wears much more suitable clothes than in her last few films. (Reference to *Garden of Allah*, *Knight Without Armor*.) Her enormous eyelashes, however, must have been a real problem for the cameraman, and when she blinks them monstrous and sinister shadows flap batlike across her curiously ascetic features.' For JVS, Dietrich's face had been the soul's mirror, to his 'successors' it meant glamour—and verged dangerously on caricature.

The films that fell between *Desire* and *Angel* were two of the most lavish productions of the time. *The Garden of Allah* (Selznick 1936) was an early Technicolor production, but the treatment of this desert romance was undistinguished. Although it cost the then staggering sum of 2,200,000 dollars, the film failed because of the mishandling of Dietrich's personality. Directors who had been clamouring for her release from Sternberg's 'stereotype' succeeded only in making her a sterotype of an infinitely worse variety. Now that Sternberg's handling of her could no longer be blamed, she bore the brunt of critics' and theatre managers' anger. She went to England early in 1937 to make *Knight Without Armor* for Korda at the then staggering fee of 450,000 dollars. It would be worth twice that sum now. (Sternberg was also at hand shooting the ill-fated *I Claudius*.) According to *World Film News*, January 1938, *Knight Without Armor* made the Russian Revolution look like a Drury Lane musical. The film was not a success; Dietrich, as the Countess Alexandra, too often looked 'curiously ascetic' when she should have seemed young and romantic. The film's famous French director, Jacques Feyder felt, 'she has great charm. She uses it with stunning virtuosity.'

Opposite:
Another bath in **Knight without Armor**

With Gary Cooper in **Desire**

Through the relative failure of these last two films she became known as a box-office liability. *Angel* failed to turn the tide, and Paramount paid her the contractual sum of 200,000 dollars *not* to make a film she had been signed for.

A plan to work with von Stroheim came to nothing, nor did she play the part in Terence Rattigan's *French Without Tears*, for which she had been announced in the autumn of 1937. In an interview Dietrich gave in Canada (*Films in Review* May 1961), she said it was on von Sternberg's advice that she made *Destry Rides Again* (1939) a Western spoof, in which she played a

Fighting Una Merkel in **Destry Rides Again**

brawling beerhall hostess, a part quite unlike anything she had played since *The Blue Angel*. It was clever casting. As the hussy with the heart of gold she regained her hold on the public's affection. Her Frenchie was a woman with a ribald sense of humour and touching warmth. Full advantage was taken of her unique and dominating personality but no attempt was made to vye with von Sternberg's 'romantic glamour'; her eyebrows were lowered, her cheekbones camouflaged with rouge. Dietrich's career was back in full swing. Throatily, she chanted some of her best songs since *Blue Angel*, and, as so often when placed

Fighting with James Stewart in **Destry Rides Again**

Fighting Broderick Crawford in **Seven Sinners**

in a rough masculine environment, she seemed eminently desirable.

The reason for the success was simple ; she had descended from the pedestal on which von Sternberg had placed her, and entered the thick of things. After *Destry* she was cast in variations on the part of Frenchie. Just as she had previously been played out as shadows of her Sternberg roles, so now she seemed to be forever essaying a mixture of hardened glamour and the Berliner song-stress.

Typical of the sort of picture her employers at Universal were casting her in was Tay Garnett's *Seven Sinners*. It was one of the best in the series, among the year's big money-makers and a film Dietrich remembers with fondness. She played Bijou, an entertainer in South Sea Island cafés, notorious throughout the US Navy.

New Statesman 1941, summed up her new-found appeal: 'In *Seven Sinners* La Dietrich sails back into her own. Not for years has she seemed so light, so alluring. . . . Singing huskily in a wonderful sailor suit, posing in black behind mosquito nets, set against sunlit lattices, carried in rickshaws and up gangways—no wonder there is a riot wherever she goes.'

Resting in **Seven Sinners**

Frederick Hollander wrote three new songs for her. Hollander may not have been a Kurt Weill or Dietrich a Lotte Lenya, but when she sang Hollander's bitter-sweet song *I've Been in Love Before*, or the rip-roaring *See What the Boys in The Backroom Will Have*, it was obvious that she was also in a class very much of her own.

Among the good follow-ups was *Manpower* (1941). It was on her hair style and make-up in this film that Stanwyck's in *Double Indemnity* was modelled. One of the worst was *Pittsburgh* (1942), a rehash of all her other stories in the series. Again John Wayne

With Franklyn Pangborn in **The Flame of New Orleans**

fought Randolph Scott over her, and a topical reference to Pearl Harbor contributed to a happy ending. In 1941 René Clair directed her in *Flame of New Orleans*, in which he aimed at the Sternberg glamour with the Destry character, spiced with Clair's own brand of humour. Dietrich did a speciality act with Orson Welles in the all-star *Follow The Boys* (1944) in which he sawed her in half. Eventually, painted in gold, she performed a harem nautch dance to end them all in the perennial 'chestnut' *Kismet* (1944). William Dieterle, who had first played opposite Dietrich in the twenties in Germany, directed her in the film. Interviewed for a

Overpage: **Kismet**

With Randolph Scott and John Wayne in **The Spoilers**

profile on her he said: 'Marlene! She's the last of the great performers. There will never again be her like, after her. Who except Marlene has been able to triumph over so many bad films?' After *Pittsburgh* Dietrich was again labelled box-office 'poison' by the American film distributors, who had applied the same judgement to stars like Garbo, Katherine Hepburn, Joan Crawford and Fred Astaire.

Opposite: Doing the 'nautch' in **Kismet**

With George Raft in **Manpower**

It would not be out of place at this point to recall the peculiar love—hate relationship that sprang up between Marlene and her native Germany early in her Hollywood career. By 1932 she was a world-famous star, and the German film industry tried to win her back. She refused. Although she could have asked any price, her revulsion for Nazism was too strong. In retaliation, *Blonde Venus* opening in Germany in November 1932 was banned in July 1933, as morally objectionable in its loose treatment of the home and marriage. But this did not prevent further attempts to woo her back for the fatherland. When she was working in England in 1937, Dietrich was approached again (some say this was at the instigation of Adolf Hitler, who used to screen *The Blue Angel* repeatedly for his private delight).

In reply she took out American citizenship in 1938. Dietrich felt so passionately about her country's position that she went to entertain troops on the allied fronts throughout Europe and

Opposite: As Fay Duval in **Manpower**

Taking her American citizenship papers in 1938

Waving her million dollar legs, she welcomes returning troops in 1945

Opposite: 'And tell them I cried'—singing *Boys in the Backroom* during one of her shows 1961

Africa, often working so close to the front lines that she risked her life. Her activities in the war were for her 'the only important thing I've ever done'. In recognition, Congress awarded her the Medal of Freedom. She entered liberated Paris with de Gaulle, who made her a Chevalier of the Legion of Honour.

Her outspoken disapproval of her countrymen's behaviour naturally made her unpopular with many Germans. In 1960 when she arrived in Berlin for her one-woman show, she was greeted with hostility in many quarters. Nevertheless, she had one of the most spectacular triumphs of her career. On her opening night there were sixty-two curtain calls. The Berlin *Tagesspiegel* wrote: 'Miss Dietrich had not faced a German audience for twenty-nine years. It was an exciting reunion, and from the first bar of her first song there was "jubilation in the hall" for this "reunion with a woman who has about her the aura of Berlin" . . . a reunion with a sound that was more than the effect of her song—it was the sound of an epoch.'

In London in 1963 to open *The Black Fox*, a documentary film, describing the rise and fall of Hitler, which she had narrated, she said, 'I am a German. My qualities are essentially German ones —good and bad. I hope more good than bad. You can't reject your whole upbringing. But I just could not endure the turn my country took.'

In 1946 she made a film in France with Jean Gabin, *Martin Roumagnac*. Dietrich had wanted to act opposite Gabin for some time and in this, her only French film, she played an unlikely small-town siren, which was not ideal material for her. Though France

With Jean Gabin in **Martin Roumagnac**

has become almost a second home for Dietrich, and the French public is among her most devoted audience, her few films with French directors did not enhance her reputation or theirs. She returned to Hollywood for *Golden Earrings* (1947) at Paramount. They announced her return to films with 'The incomparable Dietrich', and she did not fail them. For the gypsy 'wise woman', Lydia, she designed her own make-up. Covered from head to foot in a dark brown dye, wearing a greasy black wig, barefooted and long-legged, jangling heavy bracelets, golden earrings, and chewing garlic, she gave one of her most likeable characterizations.

With Ray Milland in **Golden Earrings**

She followed this up with a great personal triumph in Billy Wilder's *Foreign Affair* (1948) as Erika von Schleutow, former mistress of a top-Nazi, now seeking a black-market living in post-war Berlin as a sultry singer in a shady nightclub. Her portrayal showed that, whatever political opinions she held, she was a Berliner at heart. Again Hollander penned the songs and she sang *In the Ruins of Berlin* with a cynical durability and Teutonic 'gutsiness', that made her part live as something more than a glamorous platform for Wilder and Brackett's sardonic wit and thinly-disguised slogans.

It was an electric reminder of how fine an actress she still was. For all there was the joyous re-discovery that she was 'more lusciously seductive than she has even been, or than any screen siren has ever been.' There were more films, but this was her last personal success as a top box-office magnet in films.

She then made two films in England. *Stage Fright* (1950) was a lesser Hitchcock effort, and employed the Dietrich personality for little other than glamour. As Charlotte Inwood, musical comedy

Overpage: As Erika von Schleutow in **A Foreign Affair**

As Charlotte Inwood 'The Laziest Gal in Town', **Stage Fright**

No Highway, with James Stewart

queen, who conceals incriminating evidence in her husband's apparently accidental death, she had a Cole Porter song and lots of glamour. The role was subordinate to Jane Wyman's. Fox cleverly re-teamed her with *Destry* co-star, James Stewart, in *No Highway* (*In the Sky*) 1951. Dietrich gave an intelligent and sensitive performance as Monica Teasdale, a movie star on a flight in danger of crashing, whose thoughts turn to the value of her work and life. Director Henry Koster added his observation of Dietrich to the records : 'Marlene must be treated in the studio like a queen. But if you need Super Glamour for a part, you cannot get anybody better than her.'

Next came the fascinating, ambiguous *Rancho Notorious*, directed by her countryman, Fritz Lang. It was a most unusual

Western, replete with symbolism, such as the name of the Dietrich character, Altar Keane, mistress of the gangsters' hideout, 'Chuck-a-Luck'. Lang's obsession with Dietrich as a physical sexual image, with numerous shots of cleavage and legs, made one uncomfortably aware that she had reached her fifties. By 1952 she was best known as the world's youngest, best-looking and shapeliest-legged grandmother. She created a stir at the annual Oscar night, when, to audible gasps, she came on to accept an award for a friend, wearing a simple, full-length black dress slit

Overpage: At the Sahara Hotel, Las Vegas, in the high-kicking finale of her act 1959

As Altar Keane in **Rancho Notorious**

up to the thigh. But more often she could be seen to better advantage pushing her grandchildren through New York's Central Park than in some of the spineless filmic efforts that employed her to cash in on a name that symbolized glamour, even if few remembered why. While a new blonde star, Marilyn Monroe, who had started to become a myth in her own right, took over the film public's attention, Dietrich, back on the stage, proceeded to show everyone 'why'. She embarked on a new career that was to recapture the stature Sternberg's films had once accorded. There was an added dimension which the intervening years' experiences had added. She had always been quick to absorb what she could ; now she could project the ageless feminine myth on her own, by

Opposite: With Red Skelton and Cantinflas in **Around the World in 80 Days**

As Mme Bertholt in **Judgement at Nuremberg**

her knowledge of lighting and costume. Almost overnight she became one of the biggest lures in nightclubs and theatres. She appeared in several more films, but these were secondary to her own show. She did a guest bit in Mike Todd's all-star *Around the World in 80 Days* (1966) and another in Orson Welles's *Touch of Evil* (1958). Dressed in white she walked on in *Paris When It Sizzles* (1964) a lesson in the glamour, magnetism, and sophistication for which the film desperately strove. The difficulty in finding a part on the screen for Dietrich was solved twice more. Billy Wilder had given her the female lead in his courtroom murder mystery *Witness For The Prosecution* (1957), and she played the aristocratic widow of a German General in Stanley Kramer's *Judgement at Nuremberg* (1962). One of her best and favourite post-Sternberg roles was in the former where she played Christine Vole, the German wife of handsome Leonard Vole (Tyrone

Opposite:
Paris when it Sizzles

Touch of Evil, with Orson Welles

Power), on trial for the murder of a rich old woman. Dietrich has said of this part: 'She's not only brave, but she loves her man unconditionally. She is the kind of woman I like to play.' Richard Griffith, writing in *Image and Legend* (1959) thought that 'of all the products of her professional skill by far the most sensational was her impersonation of a Cockney woman, for this she has received far less than her due in critical praise or public appreciation.' Director Wilder gave Dietrich a flashback that was redolent of the origins of the legend. It was set in some Berlin ruins after the war (*Foreign Affair*). We see Dietrich disclosed, very Teutonically *en travestie* (*Morocco*) singing in a basement (many of her early films including *Blue Angel*); the sequence even allows for the unveiling of the famous legs when her bell-bottoms are ripped by an eager spectator. An air raid brings the *mêlée* that broke out (*Seven Sinners*) to a halt. Left alone with Power, she trades kisses and her bed for food rations (*Foreign Affair*) and lights a cigarette as only she ever could.

Opposite: Publicity photo for **Witness for the Prosecution**

With Tyrone Power in **Witness for the Prosecution**

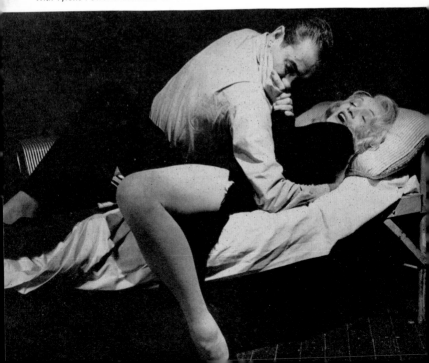

Here was the essence of all that made Dietrich a myth, and Wilder's tribute came in his conviction that Dietrich could still do it best herself.

There were rumours of a Broadway debut in a legitimate part, but they came to nothing. Dietrich once confided her wish to have played in *The Deep Blue Sea* but said that the producer had told her 'no audience would accept that a woman like Dietrich would kill herself if a man deserted her'. He explained that 'they (the audience) know that all Dietrich has to do is to stand by an open window to be instantly surrounded by hordes of men'.

'What can one say to a man like that?' Dietrich asked reflectively, 'That is the tragedy, a beautiful woman is not given an opportunity.'

In her stage act she makes her own opportunity, singing songs that allow full range to her artistry. There is a new cynicism in her voice when she sings songs about the war and Weltschmerz, and knowing longing when she sings of the pain of love, and of parting. In Jacques Brel's song, *Bitte Geh Nicht Fort* (*Ne Me Quitte Pas*) (Barclay 10278 AU and 60394 B), she has refined 'kitsch' and gives it the tragic nobility of love's last stand. She sings her songs of war like a general, weary with a painful recognition of the immutability and stupidity of it all. There is in her singing today an almost Brechtian majesty, not asking for sympathy but accusing us of apathy. With a song like *In den Kasernen* (*In the Barracks*) (Electrola E83788) which tells of

With Spencer Tracy in **Judgement at Nuremberg**

With Burt Bacharach in Moscow 1964

Overpage: Dietrich today

the soldiers, waiting in their barracks, dreaming their dreams of beautiful girls, before they are sent out to kill their fellow men, she creates a challenging atmosphere that a play like *US* sadly lacked. As once von Sternberg explored human frailty, making it palatable disguised by great beauty, so today she again looks like Venus, but speaks like a Cassandra.

Some credit for her present eminence must be given to composer Burt Bacharach. Since he first joined her troupe as conductor in 1957, he has also been her arranger and orchestrator. He shows an intrinsic understanding of the moods necessary to 'showcase' her personality. Like von Sternberg's lights, his arrangements subtly suggest the aura of romance in which Dietrich reigns supreme. There is nobody quite like Dietrich in the entertainment world today. In her sixties she still essays sex and glamour as nobody else, yet the 'Mother Courage' in her nature raises her to peaks of great art. Once, needing but not finding another director to bring out her full potential, she climbed off the pedestal. She found her Pygmalion in herself. Brushing off the dust of her travel, she climbed back up. She is unique. A tragedienne, a comedienne, singer of bawdy songs, of love and of war, she stands alone—the 'Eternal Feminine', whose infinite variety time and age have conspired to increase.

So sind die Männer (1922)
>Unverifiable title of film in which Dietrich was an extra. There are stories that she did extra work as far back as 1918.

Die Tragödie der Liebe (1923)
director Joe May
set   Paul Leni
music Löwit
cast   Emil Jannings, Erika Glassner, Arnold Korff, Wladimir Gaidarow, Ida Wust, Herman Vallentin, Guido Herzfeld, Eugen Rex, Paul Biensfeld
Mentioned by Kurt Tucholsky, 'Collected Works', Vol I, p. 1129 ff.

Der Sprung ins Leben (1923)
cast and credits unverifiable

Napoleon's Kleiner Bruder (1923)
unverifiable bit part

Der Mensch am Wege (1924)
director Wilhelm Dieterle
a still from this film in Fraenkel, 'Unsterblicher Film'

Die freudlose Gasse (So Far-Film, 1925)
director G. W. Pabst
script Willi Haas (from the novel by Hugo Bettauer)
camera Seeber, Oertel, Lach
set   Sohnle and Erdman
cast and credits in 'Illustrierter Film-Kurier' No. 199

Eine du Barry von Heute (Fillner and Somlo, 1926)
director Alexander Korda
cast   Maria Korda, Alfred Abel, Friederich Kayssler, Hans Albers
Reference in Fraenkel, 'Unsterblicher Film', p. 419. Years later, in '37, she starred for Korda in 'Knight Without Armor'

Manon Lescaut (UFA 1926)

director Arthur Robinson

script Arthur Robinson

camera Theodor Sparkuhl

set Paul Leni

cast Lya de Putti (Manon), Dietrich (Michelin), Wladimir Gaidarow, Hubert von Meyerinck, Siegfried Arno, Trude Hesterberg

story and credits in 'Illustrierter Film-Kurier' No. 412

Gefahren der Brautzeit (Hegewald Film, 1926)

director Fred Sauer

script Walter Wasserman, Walter Schlee

camera L. Schaffer

sets Max Heilbronn

cast Willy Forst, Dietrich (Evelyne), Lotte Lorring, Elsa Temary, Ernst Stahl Nachbauer, Bruno Ziener

story and credits in 'Illustrierter Film-Kurier' No. 1343

Sein grösster Bluff (Nero Film, 1927)

director Harry Piel

script Henrik Galeen

camera Georg Muschner, Gotthardt Wolff

sets W. A. Herrman

cast Harry Piel, Dietrich (Yvette), Lotte Lorring, Kurt Gerron, Vicky Werckmeier, Albert Paulig

story and credits in 'Illustrierter Film-Kurier' No. 637

Der Juxbaron (UFA, 1927)

story and cast in 'Die Filmwoche', 1Z27. Dietrich is Sophie

Wenn ein Weib den Weg verliert (Café Electric) (Sascha Film, 1928)

director Gustav Ucicky

script Jacques Bachrach (based on the stage play, *Café Electric*, by Felix Fischer)

camera Hans Androschin

cast Dietrich (Erni, daughter of the builder Göttlinger), Willy Forst, Nina Vinna, Igo Sym, Fritz Alberti, Wilhelm Voelecker

story and credits in 'Illustrierter Film-Kurier' No. 914

Prinzessin Olala (Superfilm, 1928)

director Robert Land

script Franz Schulz

camera Willi Goldberger

sets Robert Neppach

cast Dietrich (Chichotte de Gastone), Hans Albers, Walter Rilla, Georg Alexander, Carmen Boni, Ila Meery, Lya Christi

story and credits in 'Illustrierter Film-Kurier' No. 914

Ich Küsse Ihre Hand, Madame (Superfilm, 1929)

director Robert Land

camera Karl Drews, Gotthard Wolff

sets Robert Neppack

cast Dietrich (Laurence Gerard, heavy-eyed siren), Harry Liedtke, Pierre de Guingand, Karl Huszar-Puffy

cast, story, and credits in 'Illustrierter Film-Kurier' No. 1974

Die Frau nach der man sich sehnt (Three Loves: Drei Lieben) (1929)

director Curtis Bernhardt

script Ladislaus Vajda (after the novel by Max Brod)

camera Kurt Courant

cast Dietrich (Sascha), Fritz Kortner, Unno Henning, Freida Richard

Das Schiff der verlorenen Menschen (1929)

director Maurice Tourneur

camera Nikolas Farkas

script Maurice Tourneur (based on a novel by Frenzos Kerzemen)

cast Dietrich (Ethel, the Oceanflyer), Fritz Kortner, Gaston Modot, Wladimir Sokoloff, Fedor Schaljapin Jr., Boris de Fas

Liebesnächte (Strauss-Films, 1929)

The credits for this film, production and cast, are so similar to those of *Gefahren der Brautzeit* (1926) that it seems very much a re-issue under a different title, to cash in on her name.

149

Der Blaue Engel (UFA 1930)

director Josef von Sternberg

camera Günther Rittau

script Robert Liebmann and Karl Zuckmayer (based on the novel, *Professor Unrath*, by Heinrich Mann)

music Frederick Hollander and Hans Schneeberger; songs, *Ich bin von Kopf bis Fuss auf Liebe eingestellt; Lola; Nimm dich in Acht vor blonden Frau'n; Kinder, heut' Abend such' ich mir was aus* (Decca DL 8465, Capitol T 10282, Polydon 21 109EPH)

cast Emil Jannings (Professor Immanuel Rath), Dietrich (Lola Lola), Kurt Gerron, Rosa Valetti, Reinhold Bernt, Hans Albers (Mazeppa)

remade as 'The Blue Angel' with Mai Britt, 20th Century-Fox 1959

Morocco (Paramount, 1930)

director Josef von Sternberg

script Jules Furthman (based on *Amy Jolly* by Benno Vigny)

camera Lee Garmes

sets Hans Dreier

songs *What am I Bid for My Apples?*, Leo Robin
Give me the Man, Leo Robin (MFT 1172)
Quand l'Amour meurt, Millandy and Crémieux (MFT 1172)

cast Dietrich (Amy Jolly), Gary Cooper (Tom Brown), Adolphe Menjou (La Bessière), Ullrich Haupt, Eve Southern, Juliette Compton, Emile Chautard, Michael Visaroff, Albert Conti

Dishonored (Paramount, 1931)

director Josef von Sternberg

script Daniel N. Rubin, based on story by JVS

camera Lee Garmes (supervised by JVS)

sets Hans Dreier

cast Dietrich (Magda, Secret Agent X 27), Victor McLaglen (Kranau, Russian officer), Warner Oland (Colonel von Hindau), Gustav von Seyffertitz (Secret Service Chief), Lew Cody (Colonel Kovrin), Barry Norton, Davison Clark, Wilfred Lucas, Bill Powell

Shanghai Express (Paramount, 1932)

director Josef von Sternberg

script   Jules Furthman (based on an idea by JVS)

camera Lee Garmes

sets   Hans Dreier

cast   Dietrich (Shanghai Lily), Clive Brook (Captain Harvey), Anna May Wong (Hui Fey), Warner Oland (Bandit Henry Chang), Eugene Pallette (Sam Salt), Lawrence Grant (Mr Carmichael), Louise Glosser Hale (Mrs Haggerty), Gustav von Seyffertitz (Eric Baum), Emile Chautard (Major Lenard), Claude King, Allen Yung, Willie Fung

remade as 'Peking Express' with Corinne Calvet, Paramount 1951

Blonde Venus (Paramount, 1932)

director Josef von Sternberg

script   Jules Furthman and S. K. Lauren, after story by JVS

camera Bert Glennon

sets   Wiard Ihnen

songs   *Hot Voodoo; You Little So and So,* by Ralph Rainger and Sam Coslow; *I Couldn't be Annoyed,* Dick Whiting and Leo Robin

cast   Dietrich (Helen Faraday), Herbert Marshall (Edward Faraday), Cary Grant (Nick Townsend), Dickie Moore (Johnny Faraday), Rita La Roy, Sidney Toler, Cecil Cunningham

Song of Songs (Paramount, 1933)

director Rouben Mamoulian

script   Leo Birinski and Samuel Hoffenstein, based on Hermann Sudermann's novel

camera Victor Milner

songs   *Johnny; You are my Song of Songs,* Leo Robin and Ralph Rainger (Pye NPL 18113, Columbia ML 4975, WL 164, WS 316)

cast   Dietrich (Lily Czepanek), Brian Aherne (Richard Waldow), Lionel Atwill (Baron von Merzbach), Alison Skipworth (Mrs Rasmussen), Hardie Albright, Helen Freeman

The Scarlet Empress (Paramount, 1934)

director Josef von Sternberg

script   Manuel Komroff, from the diary of Catherine the Great

camera Bert Glennon

sets   Hans Dreier; Peter Ballbusch (statues), Richard Kollorsz (murals and ikons)

cast   Dietrich (Sophia Frederica, later Catherine II), John Lodge (Count Alexei), Sam Jaffe (Grand Duke Peter), Louise Dresser (Empress Elizabeth), Maria Sieber (Catherine as child), C. Aubrey Smith (Prince August), Gavin Gordon (Gregory Orloff), Hans von Twardowski, Jane Darwell, Olive Tell, Jameson Thomas, Davison Clark

The Devil is a Woman (Paramount, 1935)

director Josef von Sternberg

script   John Dos Pasos and Sam Winston, based on *The Woman and the Puppet,* Pierre Louys

camera Josef von Sternberg

sets   Hans Dreier

music   Ralph Rainger and Andres Setaro after Rimski-Korsakoff; *Three Sweethearts Have I,* Leo Robin and Ralph Rainger

cast   Dietrich ('Concha' Perez), Lionel Atwill (Don Pasqual), Cesar Romero (Antonio Galvan), Edward Everett Horton (Don Paquito), Alison Skipworth (Concha's mother), Lawrence Grant (train guard), Don Alvarado, Luisa Espinal, Hank Mann, Charles Sellon

remade as 'The Devil is a Woman' with Maria Felix, Mexico 1950; and as 'La Femme et le Pantin' with Brigitte Bardot, France 1960.

Desire (Paramount, 1936)

director Frank Borzage

script   Edwin Justus Mayer, Waldemar Young and Samuel Hoffenstein, based on a play by Hans Szekely and R. A. Stemmle

camera Charles Lang

songs *Whispers in the Dark; Awake in a Dream,* Leo Robin and Frederick Hollander

cast   Dietrich (Madeleine de Beaupre), Gary Cooper (Tom Bradley), John Halliday (Carlos Margoli), William Frawley (Mr Gibson), Akim Tamiroff (Police official), Alan Mowbray (Dr Pauquet), Zeffie Tilbury, Ernest Cossart

The Garden of Allah (United Artists, 1936)

director Richard Boleslawski

script W. P. Lipscomb, Lynn Riggs and Willis Goldbeck, based on the novel by Robert Hichens

camera Hal Rosson

music Max Steiner

cast Dietrich (Domini Enfilden), Charles Boyer (Boris Androvsky), Basil Rathbone (Count Anteoni) C. Aubrey-Smith (Father Roubier), Tilly Losch (Irene), Joseph Schildkraut (Batouch), John Carradine (Soothsayer), Lucille Watson (Mother Superior), Henry Brandon, Alan Marshal

Knight without Armor (Korda, 1937)

director Jacques Feyder

script Lajos Biro, adapted by Frances Marion from the novel by James Hilton

camera Harry Stradling

music Miklos Rosza

cast Dietrich (Countess Alexandra), Robert Donat (A. J. Fothergill), John Clements (Poushkoff), Irene Vanbrugh, Herbert Lomas, Austin Trevor, Basil Gill, David Tree

Angel (Paramount, 1937)

director Ernst Lubitsch

script Samuel Raphealson, Guy Bolting and Russell Medcraft (from the play by Melcior Lengyel)

camera Charles Lang

sets Hans Dreier

music Frederick Hollander and Leo Robin, song *Angel*

cast Marlene Dietrich (Lady Barker), Herbert Marshall (Sir Frederick Barker), Melvyn Douglas (Anthony Halton), Edward Everett Horton (Graham Valet), Laura Hope Crews (Grand Duchess Anna), Ernest Cossart, Herbert Mundin, Dennie Moore, Lionel Page

Destry Rides Again (Universal-International, 1939)

director George Marshall

script Felix Jackson, based on the novel by Max Brand

camera Hal Mohr

music Frederick Hollander and Frank Loesser, songs *L'il Joe the Wrangler; You've Got that Look that Leaves me Weak;* (See what) *The Boys in the Back Room* (will have) (Decca DL 8465, Capitol T 10282, Columbia ML 4975, WL 164, WS 316)

cast Marlene Dietrich (Frenchie), James Stewart (Destry), Brian Donlevy (Kent), Charles Winniger (Walsh Dimsdale), Mischa Auer (Boris Callahan), Billy Gilbert (Loupgenou), Irene Harvey (Janine Tyndall), Una Merkel (Lily Belle Callahan), Jack Carson (Jack Tyndall), Allen Jenkins (Bishop Watson)

remade as 'Destry' with Marie Blanchard U-I 1954

Seven Sinners (Universal-International, 1940)

director Tay Garnett

script John Meehan and Harry Tugend (based on a story by Ladislaus Fodor and Lazlo Vadnal)

camera Rudolph Mate

music Frederick Hollander

songs *I've Fallen Overboard; I've Been in Love Before; The Man's in the Navy* (Decca DL 8465)

cast Marlene Dietrich (Bijou), John Wayne (Bruce), Broderick Crawford (Little Ned), Albert Dekker (Dr Martin), Billy Gilbert (Tony), Oscar Homolka (Antro), Mischa Auer (Sasha), Anna Lee (Dorothy)

remade as 'South Sea Sinner' with Shelley Winters, U-I 1950

The Flame of New Orleans (Universal-International, 1941)

director René Clair

script Norman Krasna

camera Rudolph Mate

music Charles Previn and Sam Lerner

song *Salt O' The Sea*

cast Marlene Dietrich (Claire Ledeux), Bruce Cabot (Robert), Roland Young (Giraud), Mischa Auer (Zoloton), Andy Devine (1st sailor), Laura Hope Crews (Auntie), and Eddie Quillan, Franklin Pangborn, Melville Cooper, Gita Alpar

Manpower (Warner Bros., 1941)

director Raoul Walsh

script Jerry Wald and Richard Macaulay

camera Ernest Haller

songs Frederick Hollander, Frank Loesser

cast Marlene Dietrich (Fay Duval), Edward G. Robinson, George Raft, Alan Hale, Eve Arden, Frank McHugh

The Lady is Willing (Columbia, 1942)

director Mitchell Leisen

script James Edward Grant and Albert McCleery

camera Ted Tetzlaff

music Gordon Clifford and Jack King

song *Strange Thing* (and I find Love)

cast Marlene Dietrich (Liza Madden), Fred MacMurray (Dr Corey McBain), Aline MacMahon (Miss Budd), and Roger Clark, Arline Judge, Stanley Ridges, Ruth Ford, Kitty Kelly, Charles Lane

The Spoilers (Universal, 1942)

director Ray Enright

script Lawrence Hazard and Tom Reed (based on the novel by Rex Beach)

camera Milton Krasner

cast Marlene Dietrich (Cherry Malotte), John Wayne (Roy Glennister), Randolph Scott (McNamara), Margaret Lindsay (Helen Chester), Richard Barthelmess (The Bronco Kid), Harry Carey (Dextry), William Farnum (Wheaton) and Samuel S. Hinds, Marietta Canty

remade as 'The Spoilers' with Anne Baxter, U-I 1955

Pittsburgh (Universal, 1942)

director Lewis Seiler

script George Owen and Tom Reed

camera Robert de Grasse

cast Marlene Dietrich (Josie Winters), John Wayne (Pittsburg Markham), Randolph Scott (Cosh Evans), Louise Allbritton (Shannon Prentiss) and Frank Craven, Thomas Gomez, Ludwig Stossell

Follow the Boys (Universal, 1944)

director Eddie Sutherland

Dietrich was one of many guest stars in Universal's contribution to all-star USO entertainment films. Orson Welles, W. C. Fields, Vera Zorin, and George Raft were some of the others taking part

Kismet (Metro-Goldwyn-Mayer, 1944)

director William Dieterle

script   John Meehan (based on the play by Knoblock)

camera Charles Rosher

music   Harold Arlen and E. Y. Harburg

songs   *Willow in the Wind ; Tell me, Tell Me Evening Star*

cast   Marlene Dietrich (Jamilla, harem girl), Ronald Colman (Hafiz, the beggar), James Craig (Caliph), Edward Arnold (Grand Vizier), Florence Bates (Marsinah), and Hugh Herbert, Harry Davenport

remade as 'Kismet' with Dolores Gray, MGM 1955

Martin Roumagnac (France 1946)

(American Title, The Room Upstairs)

director Georges Lacomb

script   Pierre Very (Adapted from Pierre-René Wolf's novel)

camera Rogert Hubert

music   Marcel Mirouze

cast   Marlene Dietrich (Blanche), Jean Gabin (Martin), Daniel Gelin (School Superintendent), and Margo Lion, Jean d'Yd, Marcel Herrand, Henri Poupon

Golden Earrings (Paramount, 1947)

director Mitchell Leisen

script   Abraham Polonsky, Frank Butler and Helen Deutsch (based on novel by Yolanda Foldeso)

camera Daniel Fapp

music   Ray Evans, Jay Livingston, Victor Young

songs   *Golden Earrings*

cast   Marlene Dietrich (Lydia), Ray Milland (Col. Ralph Denistoun), Murvyn Vye (Zoltan), and Quentin Reynolds, Bruce Lester, Dennis Hoey, Ivan Triesault, Reinhold Schunzel, Hermine Sterle

A Foreign Affair (Paramount, 1948)

director Billy Wilder

script Charles Brackett, Billy Wilder and Richard L. Breen (based on an original story by David Shaw)

camera Charles B. Lang

music Frederick Hollander, *Black Market; Illusions; Ruins of Berlin; Iowa Corn Song,* and *Meadowland* (Decca DL 8465)

cast Marlene Dietrich (Erika von Schleutow), Jean Arthur (Phoebe Frost), John Lund (Capt. John Pringle), Millard Mitchell (Col. Rufus J. Plummer)

Jigsaw (United Artists, 1949)

director Fletcher Markle

Dietrich one of many 'just walk-ons' in a nightclub sequence of a second-rate thriller starring Jean Wallace and Franchot Tone

Stage Fright (Warner Brothers, 1950)

director Alfred Hitchcock

script Whitfield Cook (based on Selwyn Jepson's book *Man Running*)

camera Wilkie Cooper

music Cole Porter

song *The Laziest Gal in Town* (Pye NPL 18113, Columbia ML 4975)

cast Marlene Dietrich (Charlotte Inwood), Jane Wyman (Eve Gill), Michael Wilding (Smith), Richard Todd (Jonathan Cooper), Alastair Sim (Commodore Gill), Sybil Thorndike (Mrs Gill), Kay Walsh (Nellie), Joyce Grenfell (Shooting Gallery Attendant), Patricia Hitchcock (Chubby), Miles Malleson (Bibulous Gent), Andre Morell (Inspector Byard)

No Highway (In the Sky) (20th Century-Fox, 1951)

director Henry Coster

script Robert C. Sheriff, Oscar Millard, Alec Coppel (based on the novel by Nevil Shute)

camera Georges Perinal

cast Marlene Dietrich (Monica Teasdale), James Stewart (Mr Honey), Glynis Johns (Marjorie Corder), Ronald Squire (Sir John), Janette Scott (Elspeth Honey), Kenneth More (Dobson), Wilfred Hyde White (Fisher), Dora Bryan (Rosie), and Elizabeth Allan, Nial McGinnis, Maurice Denham, Peter Murray.

Rancho Notorious (Rank Organization, 1952)

director Fritz Lang

script Daniel Tardash (based on a story by Sylvia Richards)

camera Hal Mohr

songs Emil Newman, *Legend of Chuck-a-Luck ; Gypsy Davey;*
Get Away, Young Man.

cast Marlene Dietrich (Altar Keane), Arthur Kennedy (Vern
Haskell), Mel Ferrer (Frenchy Fairmont), William
Frawley (Baldy Gunder), and Gloria Henry, Lisa Ferra-
day, John Raven, Jack Elam, George Reeves, Frank
Ferguson.

Around the World in 80 Days (United Artists, 1956)

director Michael Anderson

producer Mike Todd

script Taylor (based on the novel by Jules Verne)

camera Lionel Lindon

cast Headed by David Niven, Cantinflas, Shirely MacLaine
and Robert Newton, it boasted one of the largest guest star cast
lists in Hollywood film making. Dietrich was the owner of a
Barbary Coast saloon, in which Frank Sinatra played the piano,
Red Skelton was a drunk, and George Raft her jealous, knife-
swinging boy friend.

The Monte Carlo Story (United Artists, 1957)

director Samuel A. Taylor

script Samuel A. Taylor (from an original story by Marcello
Girosi and Dino Risi)

camera Giuseppe Rotunno

songs *Back Home in Indiana; Rien Ne Va Plus,* and *Vogliamoci*
Tante Bene

cast Marlene Dietrich (Marquise Maria de Crèvecœur),
Vittorio De Sica (Count Dino della Fiaba), Arthur
O'Connell (Mr Hinkley), Renato Rascel (Duval),
Natalie Trundy (Jane Hinkley) Mischa Auer (Hector,
the Maître), and others.

Witness for the Prosecution (United Artists, 1957)

director Billy Wilder

script Billy Wilder and Harry Kurnitz (based on the story and play by Agatha Christie)

camera Russell Harlan

song *I May Never Go Home Anymore* (Ralph Arthur Roberts and Jack Brooks) (London Records RE-D1146)

cast Marlene Dietrich (Christine Vole), Tyrone Power (Leonard Vole), Charles Laughton (Sir Wilfrid Robarts), Elsa Lanchester (Miss Plimsoll), John Williams (Brogan Moore), Henry Daniell (Mayhew), Una O'Connor (Janet McKenzie), and Ian Wolfe, Torin Thatcher, Norma Varden, Ruta Lee, Philip Tonge, Molly Roden, Ottola Nesmith.

Touch of Evil (Universal-International, 1958)

director Orson Welles

script Orson Welles, (based on novel *Badge of Evil* by Whit Masterson)

camera Russell Metty

cast Marlene Dietrich (Tanya), Charlton Heston (Ramon Miguel Vargas), Janet Leigh (Susan Vargas), Orson Welles (Hank Quinlan), Akim Tamiroff ('Uncle' Joe Grandi), Joseph Calleia (Pete Menzies)

Judgement at Nuremberg (United Artists, 1962)

director Stanley Kramer

script Abby Mann (based on his TV play)

cast Marlene Dietrich (Mme Bertholt), Spencer Tracy (Judge Dan Haywood), Burt Lancaster (Ernst Janning), Richard Widmark (Col. Tad Lawson), Maximillian Schell (Hans Rolfe), Judy Garland (Irene Hoffman), Montgomery Clift (Rudolf Petersen), William Shatner (Capt. Byers)

Black Fox (Contemporary, 1963)

Written, produced and directed by Louis Clyde Stoumen. Narrated by Marlene Dietrich.

Paris when it Sizzles (Paramount, 1964)

director Richard Quine

The stars of this comedy were Audrey Hepburn, William Holden, and Tony Curtis. Dietrich has a guest walk-on.

Short Bibliography

Droz, Rene, *Marlene Dietrich und die Psychologie des Vamps,* Sanssouci Verlag, 1961

Frewin, Leslie, *Dietrich—The Story of a Star*, Frewin, 1967

Goetz, Alice, *Josef von Sternberg—Eine Darstellung*, Verband der Deutschen Filmclubs E.V., 1966

Lasserre, Jean, *La Vie Brulante de Marlene Dietrich,* Nouvelle Librairie Francaise, 1931

Von Sternberg, Josef, *Fun in a Chinese Laundry,* Secker & Warburg, The Macmillan Publishing Co. NY, 1965

Newspaper and magazine articles

Movie Classic, Nov. 1931 : 'Marlene Dietrich denies charge she is "Love Thief" .'

Photoplay, Jan. 1933 : 'Is Dietrich Through?', Ruth Biery ; Feb. 1932 : 'Will Marlene Break the Spell?', Kay Evans ; April 1931 : 'Dietrich—How She Happened', Otto Folischus.

Picture Play, Oct. 1932 : 'Artificial Exotics'.

Positif No. 75, May 1966 : 'Marlene Dietrich and JVS'—special issue ; articles by Louise Brooks, Robert Benayoun, John Kobal, Michel Perez, Ado Kyrou, Michel Ciment.

Sunday Times, 22 Nov. 1964 : 'I hated being a film star', Derek Prouse.

Sight and Sound, autumn 1955 : 'More Light', Josef von Sternberg.

The Times, 22 Nov. 1966 : 'A living legend, but to Marlene Dietrich it's just a bore', Elizabeth Dickson.

Die Weltwoche, 12 Nov. 1965 : 'Plus und minus eines Stars'.